IMAGES
of America

NAVAL AIR STATION
WHIDBEY ISLAND

IMAGES
of America

NAVAL AIR STATION
WHIDBEY ISLAND

William R. Stein and
the PBY-Naval Air Museum

ARCADIA
PUBLISHING

Published by Arcadia Publishing
Charleston, South Carolina

Printed in the United States of America

Library of Congress Control Number: 2017933259

For all general information, please contact Arcadia Publishing:
Telephone 843-853-2070
Fax 843-853-0044
E-mail sales@arcadiapublishing.com
For customer service and orders:
Toll-Free 1-888-313-2665

Visit us on the Internet at www.arcadiapublishing.com

Dedicated to the sailors and marines—past, present, and future—and the families of NAS Whidbey Island.

CONTENTS

ACKNOWLEDGMENTS

I am indebted to many individuals and offices for their assistance in this book, but first and foremost, I thank Kendall Campbell, archaeologist and cultural resource program manager at NAS Whidbey Island. She and Tracy Schwartz, of the same office, were cooperative (and patient) in allowing me access to information and images.

Many thanks to these fine folks as well: Marcie West of NAS Whidbey Island Public Affairs Office, who was tireless in finding old photographs; Sarah Aldrich, archivist of Island County Historical Society (ICHS)'s Janet Enzmann Archives and Research Library, who was an enthusiastic supporter of the project and went out of her way to ensure its success; Ken Worth of the National Archives (NARA) in Seattle for his aid in digging through a mountain of information; Scott Hornung for his knowledge and expertise; and, of course, the US Navy, without whose cooperation this project would not have been possible.

I am also deeply indebted to Laurin "Bud" Zylstra, a lifelong resident of the area. He is my go-to guy for local history, and a friend. Lastly, there can never be enough thanks to those whose patience was tested to the limit: my wife, Fran, and my daughter, Annika. You were the sounding board for every idea, every word, every photograph.

INTRODUCTION

Naval Air Station Whidbey Island (NASWI) has been a vital contributor to the defense of the United States for 75 years. From its beginnings in World War II until the present day, the air station has been home to a variety of aircraft that serve many purposes and missions. As time passed, the dive bombers of old gave way to jets, seaplanes were replaced in favor of more conventional landplanes, and NASWI has seen many other changes. This is its story.

The US Navy's longtime presence in Washington State came to include naval aircraft when, in 1922, NAS Seattle was commissioned on the shore of Lake Washington. Small in size, and already becoming encroached upon by the city, NAS Seattle's limitations became obvious when the Navy's new long-range patrol bomber, the PBY Catalina, arrived there in 1937. The PBY (P for Patrol, B for Bomber, and Y for Consolidated Aircraft Company) was a large aircraft for its era, and capable of carrying a wide variety of ordnance. Though a powerful weapon in the Navy's arsenal, the PBYs of NAS Seattle were eventually restricted to flying their missions unarmed due to the residential areas bordering the air base. The air station's location and size also made it an unsafe place to store that ordnance. To address these issues, Adm. Harold Stark, chief of naval operations, ordered in January 1941 that a "refueling and rearming base" be established in near proximity to NAS Seattle, but in a less densely populated area.

After examining several locations, the Navy announced in July 1941 that it had chosen an area on Whidbey Island next to the small farm town of Oak Harbor.

The chosen site was the isthmus that ties Oak Harbor to Maylor's Point. This sandy strip of land separating Oak and Crescent Harbors, both of which would be utilized for seaplane operations, was ideally suited for the Navy's needs. The news was met with mixed reactions by Oak Harbor's 350 residents. Many welcomed the economic boost the base would create, but they also knew their quiet way of life was soon to end, and for the farmers whose property would be needed, that meant leaving the land they loved.

Given its mission supporting the PBYs of NAS Seattle, Whidbey's refueling and rearming base would be strictly seaplanes and would be comprised of only 250 men and a few buildings. Surveying began in August 1941, but as the year progressed, so did plans for Whidbey's air base.

In November, it was announced that the rearming base would be its own air station, with thousands of men, and a landplane base would be included. Unfortunately, Whidbey Island's topography did not allow harbors for seaplanes and meadows for runways in the same location. The nearest suitable land for runways was in Clover Valley, some four miles from the seaplane base.

On December 7, 1941, when Japan attacked Pearl Harbor, the construction of NASWI was accelerated. Soon, there were hundreds of workers toiling on the two bases. It was already apparent that building the seaplane base would not be simple: the harbors required deepening, millions of pounds of fill dirt and gravel were needed, and the hills had to be leveled. Additionally, winter storms swept away barges and dredges. Work that had already been completed was destroyed by wind and waves. But there was a war to win, and the workers would not be deterred.

Oak Harbor became an overnight boomtown. Construction jobs were welcomed by Whidbey residents who either found employment themselves or benefited from the influx of workers from other locales. Meanwhile, those required to sell their land to the Navy were quietly packing their belongings. Many had difficulty finding new homes on such short notice. In such cases, the

Navy usually allowed people to continue residing in their former homes until they could make other arrangements.

By the summer of 1942, NASWI was nearing operational status. Construction had begun on the landplane base in March, and in a testament to wartime expediency, it was ready when Lt. Newton Wakefield landed the first aircraft there only four months later on August 5, 1942. At that time, after the completion of the runways and support facilities, naval personnel began arriving by the hundreds. The largest group of sailors were survivors from the aircraft carrier USS *Yorktown*, sunk a few weeks earlier at the Battle of Midway.

By September, Whidbey Islanders were seeing more than just sailors—aircraft were now arriving by the dozens. Clover Valley, soon to be named Ault Field, was now echoing the sounds of F4F Wildcat fighter planes. As sailors and aircraft arrived, so did official recognition. On September 21, 1942, as a Marine Corps honor guard stood by, the US flag was raised over NAS Whidbey Island. Capt. Cyril T. Simard read his orders and assumed command of the air station.

The base was still a long way from being complete. Given the tremendous effort required to build the seaplane base, it did not see the first aircraft arrive until December 1942. The Navy was also still making new land acquisitions, buying hundreds of acres along Whidbey's West Beach and transforming it into a training and target area for aerial gunners. A torpedo and bombing range was built at Lake Hancock. Eventually, the Navy acquired some 5,000 acres of Whidbey Island for various purposes, including an outlying airfield (OLF) at Coupeville in 1943. An additional field, OLF Mount Vernon (now Skagit Airport), opened soon after.

During the war, NASWI's role was manifold: defense of the Puget Sound area, training of air and ground personnel, and supporting operations in the Aleutian Islands of Alaska. The waters surrounding the island were used for bombing and gunnery practice, and the skies above Whidbey were host to a variety of aircraft, including fighters like the F4F Wildcat and the F6F Hellcat, TBF Avenger torpedo bombers, and SBD Dauntless and SB2C Helldiver dive bombers. These aircraft came and went, as dictated by the needs of the Navy, in a matter of months. The aircraft that remained at Whidbey the longest during the war years were the PV Ventura, the PB4Y Privateer, and the PBY Catalina. These aircraft were deployed from Whidbey to the Aleutians, where they operated on long-range patrols and bombing missions against the northern Japanese islands. Many of these aircraft and men never returned.

Back at home, life on Whidbey Island was changing. The tremendous influx of personnel was not limited to sailors: civilian workers by the hundreds were now employed at the base, and Navy wives and children had accompanied their husbands. Housing was at a premium, and people were forced to make long commutes or live in almost anything with a roof. Every home, apartment, room, basement, or attic in Oak Harbor was rented. Some people even lived in converted chicken houses. The waiting list for base housing seemed endless, no matter how hard supply tried to keep up with demand. Bud Zylstra, an Oak Harbor carpenter who constructed homes in base housing, recalls when he helped build an entire house in one day. Despite his labors, and those of others, the chicken houses still had tenants.

Even though housing was in short supply, recreation and entertainment were not. USO shows arrived regularly to perform at NASWI's two theaters. Movie stars, singers, and other entertainers made sure the sailors and marines of Whidbey felt appreciated. Local towns got in on the act by offering dances, tours, ski trips, and even fishing contests.

When the war ended on August 14, 1945, everything at Whidbey ground to a standstill. Deployments were halted, construction projects were cancelled, and within weeks, a steady decrease in local population began. Sailors headed home, and so did many civilians. Within months, all seaplane operations ended, and only a handful of patrol bombers remained at Ault Field. Buildings were demolished or boarded up. It seemed NASWI would, like so many other wartime naval air stations, be declared surplus and closed for good; however, this was not to be.

What made Whidbey desirable before the war was its remoteness and room for growth. In what was now the Cold War era, naval air stations would need longer runways to handle the planes of the future—jets. Whidbey, unlike NAS Seattle, could be expanded. In 1949, the Navy formally announced that NASWI would be the primary air station in the Pacific Northwest and would undergo further expansion if necessary.

The late 1940s mission of NASWI was maritime patrol. For this, a new aircraft arrived, the P2V Neptune. Highly versatile and capable of flying great distances, it would remain a fixture at Whidbey for almost 30 years. In 1950, the Korean War began, and once again Ault Field was packed with aircraft as training was conducted for aircrews to fly missions in Korea. Even the seaplane base saw a resurgence of activity, as numerous aircraft used it as a temporary training facility.

Now that NAS Whidbey was the prime air station in the region, new developments were forthcoming. In 1952, an additional runway was built that could be utilized by jet aircraft. These jets were not long in coming, but they were not what was expected; the first jets assigned to NAS Whidbey were updated versions of the P2V, which, in addition to having piston engines, were modified with two jet engines as well. The 1950s were a time of change at Whidbey, with one of the changes being the reintroduction of seaplanes in 1956. Although the seaplanes officially left in 1946, the base had remained open to transient aircraft. Now came a new squadron, VP-50, flying the P5M Marlin, and seaplane operations were once again part of daily life at NAS Whidbey. Another new sight at the seaplane base in 1956 were ships. The USS *Kenneth Whiting*, a seaplane tender, arrived and made NAS Whidbey Island her homeport. She was not to be the last; in the next 10 years, two other tenders, USS *Floyd's Bay* and USS *Salisbury Sound*, also made their homes at Whidbey.

The role of a ship that tended seaplanes included turning any harbor in the world into a seaplane base. The vessel would arrive and set up buoys for an anchorage. All the maintenance men, fuel, and parts were on the ship. After the seaplanes arrived, their aircrews would live aboard the ship. At a time when land-based patrol planes could not quite cover the oceans, the seaplane still had a valuable role to play. Another new arrival in 1956 was the A3D Skywarrior. A massive aircraft whose mission was nuclear attack, it was the first all-jet aircraft to call Whidbey home. Formed into heavy attack squadrons, the A3D was capable of operating from aircraft carriers (the largest plane ever to do so) and was the backbone of US Navy nuclear deterrence in the 1950s.

In this same era, improvements to the base reflected its growing importance. Several huge hangars were built at each end of the flight line on Ault Field. Dubbed "Miramar Hangars" by the Navy, these modern structures could house any aircraft in the naval inventory, including the P2Vs and A3Ds of Whidbey. New apartments were constructed along Ault Field's Langley Boulevard, and family homes were built near Crescent Harbor. Other changes in the 1950s included the acquisition of additional property to allow expansion of Ault Field and the construction of a naval communications site.

The 1960s brought continued growth, new aircraft, and new missions. A second runway was completed in 1962 and was a welcome addition to the base when the Vietnam War began in earnest in 1964. Whidbey aircraft were once again on the frontlines; whether they were deployed to Vietnam or to carriers, the planes and personnel of NASWI were among the first to go to the new war in Southeast Asia. Even while this was going on, new plans for Whidbey were in the works. A chapter of Whidbey's history ended when the P5Ms of VP-47 were retired in 1965. It was especially poignant in that their departure marked the end of Whidbey's original mission as a seaplane base.

Soon, a new chapter opened in the Whidbey skies: The A-6 Intruder. Designed to fly in all weather conditions and at night, the A-6 was the newest attack plane in the Navy, and NAS Whidbey quickly became the hub of their operations on the West Coast. The Vietnam War brought more men and aircraft to the station to be trained and readied for deployments to that theater. While the men were away, the base and the city of Oak Harbor made every effort to support the wives and children who anxiously awaited the return of their loved ones. For some, that return never came.

During the late 1960s and into the 1970s, the mission of the base continued to expand. The EA-6 Prowler, an electronic warfare version of the Intruder, was added to Whidbey's flight line. Another addition was the P-3 Orion patrol aircraft; however, its initial presence at Whidbey was brief, as the squadrons were deactivated within a year. The P-3 returned when VP-69, a reserve squadron commissioned at Whidbey in 1970, retired its SP-2 Neptunes in 1975. That same year marked the end of the Vietnam War, but the continuing Cold War ensured that NAS Whidbey would be busy for the foreseeable future. For the next 15 years, the air station served as the center for A-6 and EA-6 training, but when the Cold War ended in 1991, and with the A-6 fleet slated for retirement and the post–Cold War Navy having fewer aircraft carriers, plus the accompanying reductions in the military, NAS Whidbey was deemed unnecessary and recommended for closure. The future looked bleak—but not for long.

In 1993, the Navy gave Whidbey a new lease on life: it would continue flying the A-6 until that aircraft retired. EA-6 operations would continue. There would also be an expanded mission: Whidbey would now be home to all P-3 Orion aircraft on the West Coast. Soon, the Navy's top anti-submarine aircraft were arriving by the dozens. A new era had begun.

The 1990s marked new beginnings, but it was also the sunset for the venerable A-6 Intruder. When the last aircraft departed in 1997, a chapter of naval aviation history was closed. With P-3s and EA-6s, NAS Whidbey entered the new millennium only to face new challenges in the War on Terror. Deploying to Afghanistan, Iraq, and other locations, the aircraft of Whidbey Island flew countless missions, a task that continues to this day. To better cope with these new challenges, the Navy began transitioning from the EA-6 to the EA-18G Growler. Other changes for Whidbey will include the replacement of the P-3 Orion with the P-8 Poseidon.

From its humble 1942 "support base" origins, NASWI has grown to become a modern facility with over 7,000 personnel. Much has happened in those intervening 75 years, and there have been many changes. There is one constant: the US Navy and its people. Since 1942, the Navy has had a positive effect on Whidbey Island. This is reciprocated by the local community and will hopefully continue to remain a symbiotic relationship for years to come.

One

BEGINNINGS AND
THE WAR YEARS

The airplane had not been invented when this photograph was taken in the 1800s, but one day all this would become Naval Air Station Whidbey Island (NASWI). Here, Alfred Maylor poses after a hard day's work on the land that bears his family name: Maylor's Point. The flat area in the background would become a seaplane parking area, while the hill beyond was covered with housing and offices. (ICHS.)

Oak Harbor was the site chosen to refuel and rearm the PBY aircraft of NAS Seattle. With NAS Whidbey planned strictly as a seaplane facility, the twin harbors of Crescent, on the left, and Oak, on the right, were ideal for the Navy's needs. After the Navy selected this site in 1941, it soon broke ground on the peninsula and isthmus on the left. (ICHS.)

Oak Harbor, with a population of 365, soon became a boomtown as hundreds of workmen arrived to build the naval air station. The small town's lack of housing required the workmen—and, later, Navy families—to seek any available shelter. This often meant renting an attic, basement, or even converted sheds, barns, and chicken houses. (ICHS.)

Island County Times

Fiftieth Year Of Publication ESTABLISHED IN 1891

Member: NATIONAL EDITORIAL ASSOCIATION WASHINGTON NEWSPAPER PUBLISHERS' ASSN.

VOLUME XLVI — ISLAND COUNTY TIMES, COUPEVILLE, WASHINGTON, THURSDAY, JULY 17, 1941 — NUMBER 28

Huge Naval Air Station For Whidby Island

FREIMANN RESIGNS AS COUNTY AGENT EFFECTIVE AUG. 1

46 Boys and Girls Enrolled in Free Red Cross Swim Classes

ISLAND CO. ASKED TO BE REPRESENTED AT DEFENSE MEETING

LT. JOHN HIGGINS, RETIRED ARMY MAN, SUMMONED BY DEATH

Prospects Brighten For New High School At Prairie Center

PROPOSED FIELD WOULD BE BUILT BY GOVERNMENT

Four Million Dollars To Be Spent For Base Construction

The "huge" air station announced in July 1941 was a support base of only 248 men, but as the threat of war became more likely, additional money was appropriated for a fully developed air base. Before the Navy came, the locals spelled the island's name "Whidby." The official federal government name was always "Whidbey," and the Navy's influence has made this the spelling used today. (Sno-Isle Library.)

Work on the seaplane base was well underway by the spring of 1942. Wooden barracks dot the former pastures on the hillside, and the streets for naval housing are being laid. Beer's Beach, to the left, was hemmed in by a seawall and would soon be buried under a concrete parking area for seaplanes. (ICHS.)

13

Constructing the seaplane base was a major undertaking. Tons of rock were brought in to lay a foundation on the marshy isthmus. The hillsides had to be cut away and leveled. Oak Harbor, too shallow for seaplanes, was dredged and the sandy spit was sawed off to widen the harbor. On more than one occasion, high winds sank barges and undid already completed work. (ICHS.)

In this photograph of the seaplane base in the summer of 1942, the hangar is near completion, as is the control tower on the hill. The structure at right is a "nose dock" designed to ward off rain when working on an aircraft's cockpit. Most of these buildings are still in use today. (ICHS.)

As work on the seaplane base continued, construction began on the landplane base in Clover Valley on the other side of the island. Since this was already level and well-tended farmland, building the runways posed no great challenge. Although this construction began after the seaplane base was started, the landplane base was first to become operational. (US Navy.)

Before there were runways, there were cows. Clover Valley was considered the finest farmland on the island, but unfortunately for its inhabitants, it was also one of the few locales suitable for an airfield. Many existing buildings were left intact when the Navy took over. This house and barn were no exception and were converted into Navy quarters and storage, respectively. They still stand today. (US Navy.)

The landplane base in Clover Valley is pictured in 1942. Two runways are taking shape, but a number of buildings have already been constructed. Barracks were the first to go up. Newly arrived sailors, surrounded by wheat fields on an airfield yet to be built, remarked that the base looked like it had simply fallen out of the sky. Earlier arrivals had slept in barns. (US Navy.)

The contractor's barracks were the first buildings erected on the new base. This is now the site of the Sno-Isle Library. One of the men who resided in these barracks was Richard "Dick" Anable. As a dishwasher in the contractor mess hall, he received free room and board in the barracks plus $4.30 a day for loading dishes in a machine he called "The China Clipper." (US Navy.)

The landplane base was a beehive of activity as crews worked around the clock to get the base functioning. The barracks at center is now the NAS Whidbey Island post office. The large building in the background was the Combat Conditioning Center, or gymnasium. Unofficially called the "Yogi Palace" for the contortions sailors were put through to stay fit, it is the present-day gym. (US Navy.)

The first PBY Catalina arrived, and the seaplane base built to fulfill NAS Whidbey's original purpose became operational. This older type of seaplane was non-amphibious and relied on "beaching gear" to haul it in and out of the water. Several dozen sets of this equipment are lined up at the side of the hangar in anticipation of more aircraft soon to arrive. (US Navy.)

Capt. Cyril T. Simard was the first commanding officer of NAS Whidbey Island. Born in California, he became a naval aviator during World War I. After the war, he flew from the Navy's first aircraft carrier, USS *Langley* (CV-1). Additional assignments during his long career included piloting observation aircraft catapulted from battleships, as well as various command assignments. In 1941, he commanded NAS Midway Island and was promoted to captain on the spot by Adm. Chester Nimitz just prior to the Battle of Midway in June 1942. For his pivotal role in that battle, he was awarded the Navy Cross for gallantry. During his time at Whidbey, he was frequently called upon to tell his story of that battle. He retired as a rear admiral. The original administration building at NAS Whidbey, where Captain Simard had his headquarters, has been dedicated Simard Hall in his honor. (US Navy.)

With a war to be won, the Navy wasted no time in putting its newest airbase to work. Here, a PBY-5A Catalina displays its amphibious capabilities as it taxis from the waters of Crescent Harbor. Despite being ungainly in appearance, uncomfortable to fly, and very slow, the PBY made an excellent patrol bomber. (ICHS.)

A PBY-5A Catalina sits quietly in front of Hangar 17 on the seaplane base in 1945. It was one of the fastest planes in the Navy when it made its debut in 1936. Truly one of the outstanding and iconic aircraft of World War II, the Catalina served well into the jet age. (Author's collection.)

The landplane base soon became home to hundreds of aircraft of different types. Here, the parking apron is packed with PV Venturas, SB2C Helldivers, TBF Avengers, and PB4Y Privateers. It is hard to believe that just months earlier, this land was covered in fields of wheat. (ICHS.)

On August 5, 1942, Lt. Newton Wakefield became the first man to land at the new NAS Whidbey when he flew a trainer aircraft up from NAS Seattle and touched down at the landplane base. An engineer by training, Wakefield was already a key figure in the construction of NAS Whidbey, and later became its acting commanding officer in 1944. (NARA.)

Factory-fresh F6F Hellcats glimmer in the morning sun at Ault Field. Soon they would be airborne to practice dog-fighting and to strafe floating targets anchored off West Beach. There would be time for other activities as well: a rite of passage for the fledgling fighter jocks was to fly under the Deception Pass Bridge. (ICHS.)

NAS Whidbey's first executive officer was Willis B. Haviland (center). The aircraft behind him is a JRF Goose. Of note are the three different dress uniforms these men are wearing; the Navy has always had a wide array of clothing, and Haviland is wearing "Aviation Greens," which were classified as a working uniform. (US Navy.)

Comdr. Willis B. Haviland was promoted and became NAS Whidbey's second commanding officer in 1943. Haviland was a true aviation pioneer. Prior to the United States entering World War I, Haviland, having already served a hitch in the Navy, went to France as a volunteer driver for the American Ambulance Corps. When that disbanded in 1916, Haviland, still in France, took up flying. He joined the famed Lafayette Escadrille as its 16th member. This group of American volunteer pilots flew French planes and wore the uniform of that country. During that time, Haviland shot down two enemy aircraft. His later accomplishments included the first flight of a military aircraft from a ship. Shown here (on the left) in front of a SB2C Helldiver, Commander Haviland was an outgoing and well-liked skipper. As one of the most experienced pilots in the Navy, his expertise guided NAS Whidbey in its formative years. (US Navy.)

Whidbey's main mission in World War II was training aircrews for deployment to war zones. One of those areas was Alaska's Aleutian Islands, where the Japanese had invaded in June 1942. The weather proved to be a formidable foe as well. This Whidbey-based PBY is being readied for a mission on the island of Amchitka. (US Navy.)

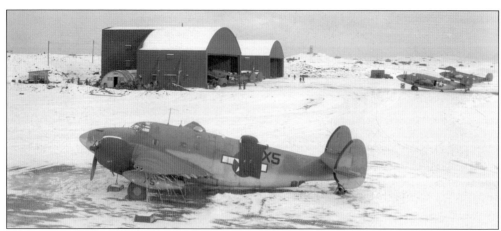

NAS Whidbey was an important part of the war in the Aleutian Islands. Here, some of Whidbey's PV-1s endure the climate of Amchitka Island while deployed there in 1945. The arctic cold tested man and machine. The PV-1, like most aircraft of the era, was not well-heated, but it was very dependable—a plus in the unforgiving Aleutian Islands. (US Navy.)

This is a view of the main gate of the seaplane base, with the hospital on the right and the gatehouse and quarterdeck on the left. Several civilian women are visible; undoubtedly workers on the base. During World War II, almost every building on NAS Whidbey was painted olive drab as a form of camouflage. The Pacific Coast was a war zone, and the base's appearance reflected this. (Author's collection.)

Despite its rather plain appearance, the control tower and operations building was the hub of activity on Ault Field. Once located on the flightline directly in front of the current administration building (Building 385), it was torn town in the mid-1950s when the current building was constructed. (US Navy.)

These air traffic controllers are hard at work in Ault Field's control tower in April 1944. With hundreds of takeoffs and landings each day, air traffic controllers had plenty to keep them busy. Also, the waters around Whidbey Island were aerial target ranges for torpedoes, bombs, and machine guns. The men in the tower had to coordinate those activities while keeping other aircraft out of the danger areas. (ICHS.)

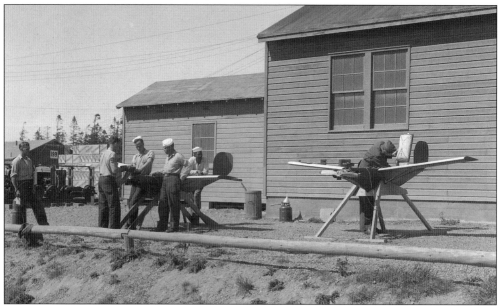

TDD radio controlled drones are readied for flight at the gunnery school on West Beach. Student gunners took aim at a variety of ground targets as well. The gunnery school closed after the war, and its land became the Gallery Golf Course. The building in the background is now the clubhouse of that course. (US Navy.)

Ault Field aviation ordnancemen are shown loading a Mark 13 aerial torpedo on a Lockheed PV-2 Harpoon in July 1945. An improved version of the PV Ventura, the Harpoon was fast, well-armed, and saw widespread use in World War II. Whidbey was home to several squadrons, as were the satellite bases at NAAS Arlington and OLF Mount Vernon. (ICHS.)

Targets for aerial and ground gunnery were towed behind aircraft like this JM-1. A variant of the Martin B-26 Marauder, the JM-1 could attain a high speed that made it ideal for such training. Given the risky nature of their business, the Navy wisely painted these planes a bright yellow to avoid the planes and their crews being shot to pieces by novice gunners. (Author's collection.)

Planned and designed before the war as a permanent installation, the seaplane base has the oldest structures built for NAS Whidbey. These venerable concrete and steel buildings contrast with the wooden buildings constructed at Ault Field in the interest of wartime expediency. The administration building (Building 12) shown here was NAS Whidbey headquarters. It now houses the Naval Heritage Center, a museum dedicated to NAS Whidbey's past. (US Navy.)

The seaplane base hangar is pictured in 1945. Years later, this was converted to house the Navy's department store, the Navy Exchange (NEX). Opened in 1977, Whidbey's NEX looks nothing like a department store on the outside and nothing like a hangar on the inside. Its parking lot is original 1942 concrete, and the mooring points for tying down seaplanes are still visible today. (Author's collection.)

The all-important weather department was housed in this building on Ault Field during World War II. Atop its tower sits a radar antenna—Whidbey was already high-tech in 1944. Despite the Puget Sound region's reputation for rain, Whidbey Island was chosen for an air station due to its generally fine weather. (US Navy.)

Buses were the principal means of transportation for NASWI sailors traveling between the two bases and the surrounding area during World War II. Here, one of those buses is being serviced by sailors on the seaplane base in front of the transportation building. This structure, still in use today, is one of the few World War II buildings at NASWI that still serves its original purpose. (Author's collection.)

OUTLYING FIELD – COUPEVILLE
U.S. NAVAL AIR STATION, WHIDBEY IS., WASH.
WHBD. NO. 2773   ALTITUDE 7930'   15 NOV. 1944

Outlying Field (OLF) Coupeville was constructed in 1943 to handle the ever-increasing volume of aircraft at NAS Whidbey. Located 10 miles from the main base at Ault Field, the OLF allowed pilots to practice their takeoffs and landings in a pattern free of interference from other aircraft. Little changed from this 1944 photograph, the OLF still serves as a valuable training aid to this day. (US Navy.)

Early morning on the 1944 Ault Field flightline saw F-6F Hellcat fighters starting engines and taxiing out for another day of training. When fully qualified, these fighter pilots would deploy to aircraft carriers in the war against Japan. One of the great fighters of the era, the Hellcat was a match for almost anything that flew against it. (ICHS.)

Sailors perform maintenance on the .50-caliber guns of a PV Ventura. One sailor uses a borescope to align the gun, while another stands by with tape to seal the end of the gun's barrel. Given the crude conditions in which the PVs had to operate, such measures were necessary to keep equipment functioning. A burst from the guns made short work of the tape. (ICHS.)

Aviation metalsmiths perform repairs to the fasteners of a life raft compartment on a Whidbey PB4Y Privateer in 1945. Dedicated and skilled men such as these were the backbone of naval aviation. Note that before they started drilling, they made sure to remove the life raft. (ICHS.)

The PB4Y Privateer was the largest plane assigned to NAS Whidbey in World War II. This patrol bomber was a huge aircraft for its time. With its wide wingspan and tall vertical stabilizer, the Privateer could not fit into any of Ault Field's hangars. Happily enough for these hard-working sailors, it was a sunny day. (ICHS.)

Ongoing improvements have made the Ault Field of 1944 almost unrecognizable today. Few of these World War II buildings remain, and the arrival of jets necessitated longer runways that replaced the two shown here. The recognizable "Main Street" of Ault Field, Charles Porter Avenue, was not built until the 1950s. (US Navy.)

AULT FIELD
U.S. NAVAL AIR STATION, WHIDBEY IS., WASH.
WHID. NO. 2770   ALTITUDE 10,200'   15 NOV 1944
200 100 0   500   1000
SCALE IN FEET

Hangar 1 on Ault Field was a bustling place in 1944. A PV-1 Ventura pokes its nose in from the right, torpedoes on trailers await loading, and a fuel truck hurries to its next job. Of Ault Field's four main hangars from World War II, only this one still stands. (US Navy.)

Patrol bombing squadron men proudly line up in front of one of their PV-2 Harpoons. At a glance, it is difficult to distinguish a Harpoon from its older brother, the Ventura. The Harpoon, however, packed three .50-caliber machine guns under its chin. Whidbey's Venturas and Harpoons spent long deployments in the Aleutian Islands, where, with their long range, they harassed the northernmost islands of Japan. (US Navy.)

PB4Y Privateers are parked wingtip to wingtip in a seemingly endless row in 1945. For planes of that era, the Privateers had a long career at Whidbey. First arriving in 1944, they remained after the war and were the main aircraft at NAS Whidbey until their departure in 1949. During the Korean War, a Privateer training squadron was activated at Whidbey from 1951 to 1953. (ICHS.)

A Navy station wagon is dwarfed by a PB4Y Privateer thundering in on short final to Ault Field in Clover Valley. The Privateers were the largest aircraft stationed at Whidbey in World War II, and for many locals, they were the biggest planes they had ever seen. (ICHS.)

A PB4Y Privateer sits in a portable hangar at Ault Field. The building in the background is well-known to anyone ever stationed at NAS Whidbey. It has undergone many name changes over the years, including "Clover Valley" and "Ault Field," but since the 1950s, its name has been the "Skywarrior Theater." (ICHS.)

The hangars at Ault Field were barely two years old when the Navy brought in planes too large to fit in them. Hangar 4 was no bigger than its three other counterparts, and the 110-foot wingspan of the PB4Y Privateer posed a bit of a problem. (US Navy.)

Another NAS Whidbey aircraft was the famous SBD Dauntless dive-bomber. Here, several squadrons in three-ship echelons go out for a drive over the San Juan islands. Large formations such as these were typical in World War II. The Dauntless was a real ship-killer during the war. Among its other achievements, this aircraft sank four Japanese aircraft carriers at Midway in 1942. (US Navy.)

Chief petty officers and sailors of the utility plane squadron proudly pose in 1944. Despite their casual appearance, several of the chiefs, when not overseeing the maintenance of squadron aircraft, flew planes themselves. These enlisted pilots were commonplace before, during, and after World War II. The last enlisted Navy pilot retired in the early 1980s. (Author's collection.)

34

A sailor on Ault Field refuels a rather weather-beaten PV-1 Ventura. This aircraft was likely a veteran of deployments to the war zone of the Aleutian Islands. When the aircraft were too war-weary for future front-line service, they were assigned training duties after they returned to Whidbey. (US Navy.)

The Bachelor Officer's Quarters (BOQ) at Ault Field was located off Langley Boulevard atop the hill overlooking the field. Torn down in the 1960s, its abandoned tennis court remains near the former site. An almost identical structure was on the seaplane base where the Navy Lodge now stands, but it was torn down when World War II ended. (Author's collection.)

The staff of the BOQ kept the place running and shipshape. The BOQ was more than just a place to live; it was also home to the Officer's Club. These chief petty officers are officer's stewards and wear the short-lived grey dress uniform. No matter what job they were assigned, they were first and foremost sailors. (US Navy.)

On the right side of the hill driving up Langley Boulevard, there were once dozens of houses comprising a neighborhood that was home to hundreds of Navy personnel and their families. All these homes were torn down when newer housing was built, but the hillside is still terraced where they once stood. (US Navy.)

What Ault Field's housing lacked in aesthetics it made up for in charm and coziness. Those who lived there have fond memories of their little hilltop community. When new homes at Crescent Harbor housing opened in the early 1960s, that was the end of this neighborhood. (US Navy.)

Very little remains of this community that once overlooked Ault Field. The buildings at lower right were multi-family houses. There were another two dozen homes not shown here. The BOQ is at top left, its tennis court behind it. The two buildings at lower left housed celestial navigation training simulators. (Malcolm Barker.)

There was never enough housing for Whidbey sailors serving in World War II. These prefab buildings were located on the present-day site of Olympic View Elementary School. Commonly mistaken for Quonset huts, these homes were actually known to the Navy at that time by the curious name "Homoja Huts." (US Navy.)

The Ault Field Infirmary is pictured here in 1945. The main hospital was located on the seaplane base, but it made sense to have a smaller version on Ault Field. This building has served many purposes over the years. It now houses the Judge Advocate General, the legal offices of NAS Whidbey. (US Navy.)

This large and sprawling building was the galley at Ault Field. Constructed in 1942, it fed thousands of sailors three times a day before it was replaced in the mid-1950s. Like many of NAS Whidbey's World War II buildings, the galley had a long life. It was the site of many different offices and served the Navy well before it was torn down in 2010. (US Navy.)

Eight of these wooden barracks were built at Ault Field in 1942. Several of them remain in use today as offices. Another seven identical barracks were atop the hill overlooking the seaplane base. When the war ended and the population of NAS Whidbey dwindled, those barracks were quickly torn down. (US Navy.)

The tower on the base operations building was barely three years old when a new one was built in 1945. The reason was simple: air traffic controllers could see the runways from the tower, but not much else. With Ault Field's numerous hangars obstructing the view, the need for a taller tower soon became evident. Throughout the war, the tower was identified over the radio as Clover Valley Tower. (US Navy.)

PBYs did not always fly out of the seaplane base, as these lined up in front of Hangars 2 and 3 in early 1945 attest. Designed in the 1930s, when large planes lacked proper runways, the PBY seaplane reflected those times. During World War II, runways were built everywhere, and the need for seaplanes diminished. Amphibious PBYs typically used a runway when available. (ICHS.)

An aircraft mechanic in World War II spent most of his time working on one part of the plane, and that was its engines. The massive reciprocating motors of the PB4Y Privateer were no exception. NAS Whidbey did more than just train aircrews; it established schools for all aspects of aircraft maintenance, a mission that continues to this day. (ICHS.)

There was more than one way to start a PBY. The airplane carried handles to crank a flywheel should the regular engine starter fail—a common occurrence with the technology of the time. As this photograph shows, it was usually a two-man job. It was also a good practice to have a fire extinguisher–wielding sailor nearby. The "loop" is a radio direction-finding antenna. (US Navy.)

NAS Whidbey's Hi-Flyers were an extremely popular swing and jazz ensemble during World War II. They did more than play at the base; they were also in high demand at various functions all across the Pacific Northwest. NAS Seattle's band, the Jive Bombers, were the Hi-Flyers' only serious competition. (ICHS.)

A Whidbey sailor putting the "hi" in "Hi-Flyers" demonstrates that the band members had other talents besides playing popular music. The Hi-Flyers' reputation for putting on a good show was well deserved. Besides their reputation as quality musicians, they were also well respected for their singing. (ICHS.)

Boys will be boys, and one thing will never change: sailors are willing to do anything for a laugh. With a theater on Ault Field and another on the seaplane base, Whidbey sailors never lacked for movies or live entertainment. Risqué (or just plain silly) routines were part of the show. Several USO shows at Whidbey brought in movie stars and popular bandleaders. (ICHS.)

The seaplane base gatehouse hosted a number of offices, as well as the shore patrol and a jail for rowdy sailors. Bad behavior was usually punished by restriction to the base. Restricted sailors were known to bypass the gatehouse at night and sneak into town via the beach. The shore patrol learned to look for sailors with muddy shoes. (US Navy.)

This 1945 photograph was taken from the porch of one of the barracks near the Victory Homes housing area. Numerous PBYs are visible, as is the boathouse at center left. The scene has changed over the years, but the view today would be very similar to this. (Author's collection.)

This ordinary looking building was home to a branch of the NAS Whidbey Commissary. Located in what is now Victory Terrace housing, this store was ideally situated. The main commissary was much larger, but the one shown here was easier to get to and was referred to by housing residents as "the country store." (US Navy.)

The NAS Whidbey commissary staff of World War II was comprised entirely of naval personnel. Most of the sailors who worked there were trained and rated as cooks, and part of a cook's job might entail working in the Navy-run commissary. The main commissary was located in the basement of Building 13. (US Navy.)

Although it was located under the same roof as the main galley for NAS Whidbey, the snack bar, or "Gedunk," in Building 13 was a favorite gathering place for Whidbey sailors and civilian workers. There was nothing wrong with Navy chow, but if one wanted a milkshake, or wished to linger over a cup of coffee, the Gedunk was the place to do it. (US Navy.)

Whidbey's West Beach was home to a number of Navy facilities. Rocky Point (near the top of this photograph) was the location of a radio transmitter and observation post, but the main function of this area was as the Gunnery School for aerial and ground gunners. The geometric shapes are berms that shielded the equipment used to pull the targets. Student gunners on trolley cars were towed along the diagonal road (at center) while firing at the targets. The rifle and pistol range is located to the south of the berms. It was later moved a half-mile north, and its site was given to the state for the creation of Joseph Whidbey State Park. Most of the gunnery school land is now a golf course. Several World War II buildings on the site are still in use, including the trolley storage building (clubhouse) and the guardhouse (restrooms). (US Navy.)

Training for aerial gunners was realistic in that aircraft gun turrets were utilized at the gunnery range. Towed on rail cars along West Beach, the gunners fired at targets behind earthen berms near the water's edge. The berms are still present, as is the road in the foreground—it is now the entrance to NAS Whidbey's small arms range. (NARA.)

A PBY-5A taxis into a calm Crescent Harbor. If the water was too smooth, the aircraft could not break the surface tension on takeoff, and a boat would be used to rough up the waters. Although the aircraft is afloat, it was common practice to leave the wheels down to act as a keel. (ICHS.)

The seaplane base in 1944 was a hive of activity. Close examination reveals PBY seaplanes, housing, barracks, the torpedo shop, the boathouse, a hangar, the laundry, and the equipment used by aircraft beaching crews. The large building on top of the hill was a theater. (US Navy.)

Naval personnel and civilians inspect a PBM Mariner at Whidbey's September 1945 open house. The war had ended only days earlier when NASWI opened its doors to the local community, and for many, this was the first time they saw what went on at this base that only four years earlier had not existed. (ICHS.)

PBM Mariners are shown lined up in 1945. A newcomer to NASWI that same year, the PBMs did not replace the older PBYs, but those aircraft, being amphibious, could operate from Ault Field's runways. This made room for the PBMs to take over the seaplane base, as shown here. (ICHS.)

The PBM was a very large aircraft, but the cockpit area was like a cramped office. The PBM had great endurance, and the pilots, navigator (left), and radioman (right) called this space home for up to 18 hours at a time. The aircraft also had a large number of crewmen not visible in this photograph. (US Navy.)

The seaplane base had grown tremendously since 1942, and by 1945, it was a modern naval air base. The base now dwarfed the town of Oak Harbor, which, despite a surge in population, was still fairly small. Materials for civilian homes were scarce during World War II, so Oak Harbor's new residents were squeezed into existing homes for the most part. Aircraft are visible on both ramps of the seaplane base, but most flying activity took place on Crescent Harbor, as illustrated by the PBY taxiing in the water. Maylor Point is somewhat barren, but the BOQ and the commanding officer's home were both located near the woods. (US Navy.)

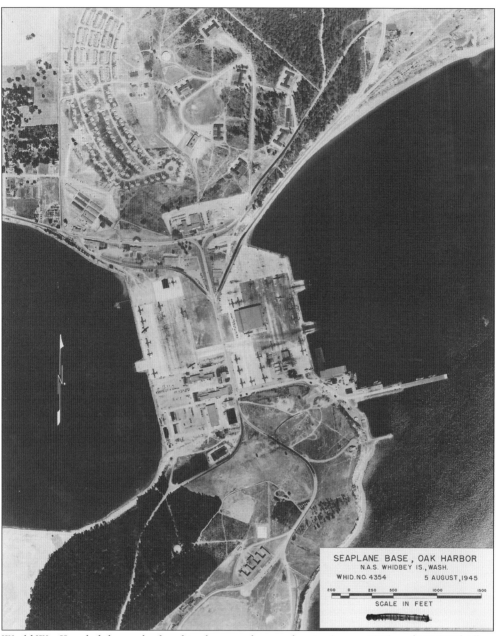

SEAPLANE BASE, OAK HARBOR
N.A.S. WHIDBEY IS., WASH.

WHID. NO. 4354   5 AUGUST, 1945

SCALE IN FEET

World War II ended the week after this photograph was taken in August 1945, and NAS Whidbey Island's future—like that of many wartime military bases—was uncertain. However, the Navy was already examining the situation, and for the same reason NAS Whidbey was built it was retained as an active air base, but only as a landplane facility. Seaplane usage rapidly dwindled in the postwar years. Advances in runway construction and landplane aircraft design helped to elbow the landplanes' aquatic cousins out of the picture. The seaplane base was used for a very short time after the war, then placed in caretaker status. Other than the Navy housing, the base was a mere shadow of its wartime self. The hangar sat empty and silent and the wooden BOQ and barracks were soon torn down, but the base had accomplished its mission. (US Navy.)

Two

COLD WAR SENTINEL

A symbol of NAS Whidbey's growth to come, a P2V Neptune of Patrol Squadron 9 (VP-9) leaps into the sky at Ault Field in 1949. Now that NAS Whidbey was a permanent installation, and the Cold War had begun, the base would see expansion matched only by its initial development less than 10 years earlier. (US Navy.)

In the immediate postwar era, World War II airplanes remained the norm at NAS Whidbey. The seaplane base still hosted PBMs, as shown here in a 1946 photograph taken from a PBM at anchor in Crescent Harbor. At the foot of the slipway is a tractor nicknamed "Lulubelle" used for handling the aircraft. (Lesley Bond.)

A PB4Y Privateer cruises over Ault Field in 1946. This photograph, taken by Ens. Malcolm Barker, a navigator in VPB-120, shows Ault Field as it looked for its first 10 years. The diagonal strip of concrete adjacent to the taxiway at left center was used for sighting-in and testing machine guns—aircraft would be tied down and fire their guns into a backstop at the end of the strip. (Malcolm Barker.)

Doris Barker, wife of Ens. Malcolm Barker, smiles for the camera in 1946 from the hilltop housing overlooking Ault Field. With World War II over and the Korean War yet to come, life at NAS Whidbey in those interwar years was relatively calm and pleasant. The land at the bottom of the hill was later acquired by the Navy. (Malcolm Barker.)

Off-duty activities with friends has always been an important part of Navy life—no matter what the era. Taking advantage of a sunny afternoon, these men from VPB-120 relaxing with their wives (and babies) along the shores of Whidbey Island in 1946 are participating in activities very similar to those of their present-day counterparts. (Malcolm Barker.)

Heavy snows and rains caused severe flooding at Ault Field in 1949. Most of the aircraft, like these PB4Ys in front of Hangar 3, were moved to higher ground. The theater sits high and dry at center. The flooding was a reminder that Ault Field had been hastily laid out in wartime, but now, as part of a permanent base, it would need improvement. (US Navy.)

With the Navy's maritime reconnaissance role evolving from using seaplanes to more versatile landplanes, the arrival of the P2V Neptune in 1949 ushered in a new era at NAS Whidbey. The outbreak of the Korean War the following year saw an upsurge in combat crew training as the Neptune squadrons deployed to the Far East in what was now the hottest spot in the Cold War. (US Navy.)

A snowy morning at Ault Field meant de-icing the Neptunes of VP-4 in preparation for another day of training. The Neptune has the distinction of being the Navy's only land-based patrol aircraft designed and built as such, with all others being modifications of existing aircraft designs. (US Navy.)

Training aircrews at NAS Whidbey for the Korean War meant time spent on simulators such as this top-turret trainer in Building 126 at Ault Field. The .50-caliber guns of the Neptune were frequently needed to defend the aircraft as they flew hazardous reconnaissance missions on the coast of North Korea and China. Several Whidbey P2Vs were lost during the war. (US Navy.)

The Korean War had scarcely ended when, in 1955, there began a major upgrade to NAS Whidbey. Hangars were constructed, roadways built, and barracks and support buildings were erected—a reflection of NAS Whidbey's importance to the Cold War–era Navy. Land was cleared, the nose docks on the right were soon gone, and Hangar 6 was built in their place. (US Navy.)

As P2Vs wait expectantly in the background, the foundation of Hangar 6 was laid in 1955–1956. This modern steel-and-concrete structure served NAS Whidbey well and remains in service to this day. In the foreground, the earth is being leveled for another major project: a thoroughfare that would serve as a main road for Ault Field. (US Navy.)

At the north end of the Ault Field flightline, Hangar 5 was built. A new control tower and half of the hangar were already in use in this 1956 photograph. The remainder of the structure was completed later that year. This was the Navy's new "Miramar Hangar" type, which is still in use today. (US Navy.)

Another view of Hangar 5 while under construction in 1956 shows the gym and West Beach in the background. The smoke emanating from the beach came from the base garbage dump. In those times, the rubbish from NAS Whidbey—like many other places—was simply dumped along the water's edge and burned. (US Navy.)

A much-needed addition to NAS Whidbey was its new "Main Street," later named Charles Porter Avenue. The street was named in honor of Comdr. Charles S. Porter, a World War II hero and commanding officer of Heavy Attack Squadron Two (VAH-2) who lost his life while piloting an A3D in 1960. (US Navy.)

Another major addition to NAS Whidbey—and a very welcome one at that—was the construction of these modern concrete and steel barracks. Completed in 1954 and designed to house 300 men each, these buildings, with extensive renovations and upgrades, are still home to many sailors today. (US Navy.)

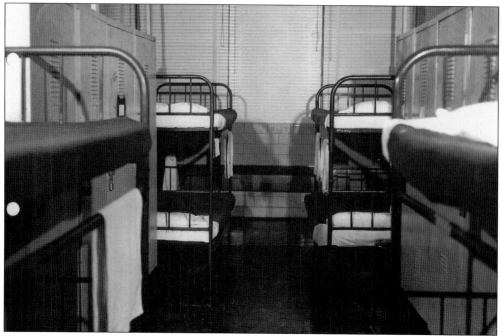

What the new barracks lacked in luxury they more than made up for in comfort and warmth. Although the interior looks decidedly austere, this was the accepted living environment of the Navy at that time. The sailors were glad to have solid walls, a recreation room, and hot showers. (US Navy.)

A showpiece at NAS Whidbey, the new barracks were a source of pride for those used to living in the crowded and drafty wooden barracks that had been home to Ault Field sailors since 1942. Another new addition was the modern galley at left. These facilities are still in use today. (US Navy.)

The mid-1950s saw new barracks being built, but NAS Whidbey still needed to address its lack of base housing. For a number of years, a trailer park was the only option for married sailors and their families. Located along Simard Street (now Regatta Drive), this trailer park served its purpose until the Navy built new housing in the 1960s. (US Navy.)

This 1954 image shows new base housing in the form of the Whidbey Apartments at center left. Above them are the two navigator training simulator buildings, the BOQ, and (climbing the hillside to the right) housing for officers. The land to the right of the apartments and below the housing had yet to be acquired by the Navy. (US Navy.)

When NAS Whidbey skipper Capt. William Galley departed in 1953, he went in style. Side boys lined the seaplane base's Coral Sea Avenue as the captain and his family bid farewell to Whidbey. The sailors trace the route Captain Galley will take as he departs. At that time, the base was accessed via a gate on what is now Pioneer Way. (US Navy.)

The 1950s also saw the addition of a new headquarters, or administration building. Completed in 1955, Building 385 (the "White House") has been the center of NAS Whidbey command facilities ever since. Even with a few more recent additions, the building is still easily recognizable today. (US Navy.)

NAS Whidbey's chapel was relocated in the 1950s to a leftover World War II–era building, but that was a far cry from the earlier days when chapel was held in barracks, the theater, or the administration building. This was not much of an issue, because as current NAS Whidbey chaplain Lt. j.g. Edwin Handley states: "Chapel can be held anywhere; it is not the building that matters." (US Navy.)

Marines line up for inspection on the seaplane base in 1954. The Marine detachment at NAS Whidbey guarded the base, manned the gates, and also took part in overseas deployments. Long a part of the base's history, marines have served as aircrew and maintenance personnel and performed a host of other functions. (US Navy.)

Marines stand at attention while being inspected in their barracks in Building 13 on the seaplane base. Many of the marines of that era were veterans of World War II and the Korean War. Duty at NAS Whidbey was a welcome respite from the rigors of combat, but Marine standards never waver regardless of their duty assignment. (US Navy.)

A rescue boat cruises the waters of Crescent Harbor in the 1950s. NAS Whidbey was home to a small fleet of these boats, which acted as rescue craft and as security for patrolling the waters around the base. Operating from the boathouse once located on the seaplane base, these vessels rescued both downed airmen and civilians in distress. (US Navy.)

Even when perched in the pilot's seat of a P2V Neptune, a military working dog never truly enjoys a relaxing life. It is doubtful this German shepherd, a part of the Marine detachment at NAS Whidbey, is as amused by his situation as the people around him. (US Navy.)

Three

MARITIME PATROL AND HEAVY ATTACK

A new era dawned at NAS Whidbey when the A3D Skywarrior arrived in 1956. The coming years would bring many changes to Whidbey—some new, some a return to the base's original mission. In this image, a Whidbey-based A3D of VAH-4 is being marshalled into position on the USS *Hancock*. (US Navy.)

The new era dawns as an A3D of VAH-4 joins up with a P2V of VP-2 over Ault Field in the late 1950s. A new runway was added a few years before—just in time for the A3D. A huge and heavy aircraft whose main purpose was delivering a nuclear bomb, a fully-loaded A3D lining up for takeoff used every inch of available runway. (US Navy.)

Seaplanes, the basis of the original mission of NAS Whidbey, returned in 1956 with the arrival of VP-50 and its P5M Marlins. When its planes departed in the late 1940s, the seaplane base had remained open for visiting aircraft, but now it was once again fully operational. The small, box-like building in the foreground was used for storage of the aircraft's machine guns. (US Navy.)

Each aircraft carried a large number on its nose identifying the plane as "8 Boat," "5 Boat," etc. The flying boat crews were a breed apart and referred to themselves as "Smooth Water Sailors." The control tower overlooks the ramp, and the seaplane tender USS *Kenneth Whiting* (AV-14) is moored at the pier; NASWI was its homeport from 1957 to 1958. (US Navy.)

Another seaplane tender homeported at NAS Whidbey was the USS *Floyds Bay* (AV-40). A tender could turn any harbor into an airbase. Loaded with aircraft fuel and parts, the vessel would set up an anchorage, the planes would arrive, and the aircrews and maintenance men would live aboard ship. Tenders were heavily armed to enable them to defend the anchorage. (US Navy.)

An A3D pilot from VAH-4 gives a thumbs-up for the camera as he readies for departure from NAS Whidbey. Despite its enormous size, the A3D crew consisted of only three men: pilot, bombardier-navigator, and navigator-gunner. Later variants of the aircraft had larger crews for the A3D's ever-evolving missions. (US Navy.)

NAS Whidbey's A3Ds lost no time in deploying for operations with the fleet. Here, an aircraft from VAH-8 launches from the USS *Lexington* in August 1958. With its heavy weight, the A3D needed considerable speed for takeoff. Aircraft carriers would ring up for maximum speed to assist the Skywarriors with getting airborne. (US Navy.)

The Ault Field flightline in the early 1960s was a busy place. Now home to dozens of A3Ds that comprised several Heavy Attack Squadrons, NAS Whidbey was a hub of excitement and activity. Given the needs of the Skywarrior, plans were already in place for additional parking space and another runway. (US Navy.)

A group of aircraft maintenance personnel from Heavy Attack Two pose with one of their charges after graduation from an A3D training course. Throughout its long life, the Skywarrior, big and complicated as it was, required extensive maintenance to stay in the air. (US Navy.)

An immaculate TA-3 of VAH-123 is on display at NAS Whidbey's AirFair open house in the early 1960s. The aircraft was spotless for a good reason: It had been modified into a VIP transport complete with airline seats, tables, and a galley. P-2 Neptunes of VP-1 are lined up in the background. (Author's collection.)

By the mid-1960s, the Skywarrior was part of everyday life at NAS Whidbey, but with one small difference. In 1962, the Navy adopted the US Air Force's system for identifying aircraft. The manufacturer's suffix was dropped, and the A3D (attack, third type, from Douglas Aircraft Co.) was renamed the A-3. All Navy aircraft were affected by this change. (Author's collection.)

Newer aircraft were arriving, but the patrol squadrons flying the P2V continued to play a major role at NAS Whidbey. Here, a P2V mechanic tends to one of the aircraft's powerful Wright R-3350 reciprocating engines. To improve the aircraft's performance, two jet engines were added in the 1950s. (US Navy.)

The Neptune's jet engines were used primarily for takeoff and climbs. Even so, the two Westinghouse J34 jets were sufficiently powerful to maintain level flight even if the reciprocating engines were shut down. Because the jets burned far more fuel than their reciprocating brethren, shutting down those engines in flight was not recommended procedure. (US Navy.)

The hunter and the hunted. A submarine periscope view of a snooping P2V illustrates the cat-and-mouse game that is anti-submarine warfare. The P2V was redesignated P-2 in 1962 when the Navy adopted the Air Force's aircraft designation system. Other Whidbey aircraft affected were the A3D (A-3) and the P5M (P-5). (US Navy.)

The aircrews of these VP-1 P2Vs got a good look at Seattle's Century 21 Exposition/World's Fair in 1962. During the World's Fair, buses ran daily between NAS Whidbey and downtown Seattle to transport sailors and their families to enjoy the fun. The Navy had an exhibit booth that was frequently manned by Whidbey sailors. (US Navy.)

A group of local businessmen watch as a P5M of VP-47 taxis across Crescent Harbor prior to take-off in the early 1960s. Public relations have always been an important subject for the US Navy. By demonstrating its aircraft and the missions they perform, the Navy bridges any knowledge gap that may exist between itself and the public, especially the local populace. (Author's collection.)

A P5M-1 from NAS San Diego's VP-40 pays a visit to NAS Whidbey in 1957 as the beaching crew prepares to recover the aircraft. With no landing gear whatsoever, the Marlin had to choose its routes accordingly. Flying overland was not the first option, but it was unavoidable. Lakes and other bodies of water were already mapped out in case of an emergency. (US Navy.)

A group of Royal Canadian Navy cadets disembark at the seaplane base after flying in from their home country via a P5M Marlin. Only a few minutes by air from NAS Whidbey Island, and visible from its shores, Canada has a long tradition of teamwork with the US Navy. Canadian sailors are stationed here and work hand-in-hand with their American counterparts. (Author's collection.)

A P5M of VP-47 pays a call at NAS Whidbey in the late 1950s. This squadron transferred to Whidbey in 1960. A typical beaching crew consisted of eight or nine men, and handling a plane this size could be a delicate operation—especially in weather conditions not as favorable as those shown here. (US Navy.)

An aircraft the size of a Marlin required heavy-duty beaching gear. The box-shaped devices are flotation chambers for when the airplane cast off its wheels. After an aircraft departed, the beaching crew would haul the beaching gear from the water, inspect it, then ready it for the aircraft's return. (US Navy.)

This ungainly looking NAS Whidbey–based ship served a critical role in seaplane operations as a salvage vessel, tugboat, and—when debris cluttered the runway/harbor—a driftwood sweeper. The boat on the left was fitted with a bumper and was used as transport to planes on the water; it was painted orange and carried a United States aircraft insignia on its bow. (US Navy.)

The role of the P5M Marlin was maritime reconnaissance. Although anti-submarine patrols were a large part of that role, the task of identifying ships, watching for smugglers, patrolling enemy coasts in wartime, and conducting search-and-rescue missions were all part of a seaplane crew's life. (US Navy.)

A typical P5M patrol could make for a very long day. Many hours were spent scanning the ocean's surface. Although loaded with sophisticated radars and sensors, maritime patrol aircraft still place reliance on the human eye. This is especially true during search-and-rescue operations. (US Navy.)

Parked inside what is now the Navy Exchange, a P5M Marlin of VP-47 plays host to a group of visiting schoolchildren in the early 1960s. For these schoolgirls, this may have been their first look inside a P5M, or perhaps their first time inside an aircraft at all. (Author's collection.)

This gate on Langley Boulevard was a familiar sight to Whidbey Islanders for many years. Once located at the top of the hill near Ault Field, the gate was moved to its current site (shown here) in the 1950s. The warehouse in the background is still in use today. (US Navy.)

One of the additions to NAS Whidbey during the 1950s was the transmitter site located near the golf course. Formerly perched on a bluff at Rocky Point, the new transmitter station was built on the grounds of the World War II gunnery school range. The berms in the foreground once shielded the target-towing equipment. Gunners on a small train car moved along the parallel road. (US Navy.)

With its establishment as a postwar permanent base, NAS Whidbey acquired additional land in the 1950s. The farm in the foreground is now home to the firefighting school. The land to its left is now the site of the Naval Hospital. All of the structures in the foreground were eventually razed. (US Navy.)

A close-up shows details of the housing area that formerly stood near the intersection of Langley Boulevard and Ault Field Road. Clover Valley Elementary School is left of center. When the Navy took title to the land in the foreground and center, a new gate was opened on what became Saratoga Street. (US Navy.)

Clover Valley Road was later renamed Ault Field Road, and in the 1950s, it was not the long and straight thoroughfare of today. When the road was improved in the early 1960s, it cut through the triangle of roads shown here. Traces of the original road can still be found in the woods parallel to the modern street. (US Navy.)

Runway 12/30 was a veteran of Ault Field. Built in 1942, by the 1950s, it was no longer adequate for the Navy's needs, and a new runway was proposed to accommodate the A3D attack aircraft. The former Runway 12 is still used today as a taxiway. (US Navy.)

U.S. NAVAL AIR STATION
WHIDBEY ISLAND
AULT FIELD
NEW 8000' RUNWAY
DELINEATED AND SUPERIMPOSED
ON AERIAL PHOTO BY HAL WEST
MAY 1960

The newest runway at Ault Field, Runway 13/31, opened for business in 1962. With dimensions of 8,001 feet by 200 feet, it and the intersecting Runway 7/25 continue to serve as NAS Whidbey's runways. Runways are named for their compass bearing, and 13/31 was later readjusted and named 14/32. (US Navy.)

In 1960, VP-50 departed from Whidbey, and VP-47 arrived from NAS Alameda. The squadron was deployed when this photograph was taken in 1964, leaving only one aircraft and an oil-stained tarmac to mark their presence. The L-shaped building at the water's edge was the boathouse for the various small craft that supported seaplane operations. (US Navy.)

Hangar 17 served its original purpose for almost 30 years. In the early 1960s, it was the venue for this group of local businessmen as they toured a P5M from VP-47. Now, this portion of the former hangar is where Navy Exchange customers pick up large items and layaways. The main barracks and galley (Building 13) overlooks the scene from the hillside beyond. (US Navy.)

This "9 Boat" of VP-47 illustrates the enormity of the P-5. The massive beaching gear is clearly visible, as is one of the aircraft's two bomb bays opened for loading or inspection. Ordnance was ingeniously stored in these bays, which were part of the nacelles that housed the engines. (US Navy.)

Another of NAS Whidbey's seaplane tenders was the USS *Salisbury Sound* (AV-13). Arriving in 1963, the "*Sally*," a Currituck-class tender, was capable of supporting two 15-plane squadrons and housing 320 squadron members. The *Sally* made several deployments to Vietnam and was homeported at NAS Whidbey from 1963 until her decommissioning in 1967. (US Navy.)

One of the advantages of a Currituck-class vessel was its ability to carry two aircraft on its aft deck. The planes were not typically carried there but were hoisted aboard for maintenance that could not be performed when the plane was in the water. P-5s carried platforms and scaffolding that enabled mechanics to perform routine maintenance while the aircraft was afloat. (US Navy.)

As US involvement in the Vietnam War escalated, so too did A-3 training and operations at NAS Whidbey. Skywarriors of VAH-4, as shown here, were called upon to make frequent deployments to southeast Asia, where they served in the role of conventional bombers and attack aircraft. (US Navy.)

The sheer size of the A-3 made it an attention-getter on any given day, and especially at airshows and open houses. "The Whale," as it was affectionately known, was not an easy aircraft to handle, particularity when landing on an aircraft carrier. The plane would slam down and then bounce and wallow about the deck in what was termed the "whale dance." (Author's collection.)

Since the 1950s, the Navy's aerial demonstration team, the Blue Angels, have been frequent visitors to NAS Whidbey Island. When this photograph was taken in the early 1960s, the Blue Angels were equipped with the F11F Tiger seen at left. The team's support aircraft are at center: the big R5D transport and the TF9J Panther used for training and VIP rides. (Author's collection.)

The A-3 was an excellent aircraft partly because it was highly adaptable to the Navy's ever-changing requirements. One such adaptation was one that transformed many A-3s for the aerial refueling role; with its own large fuel capacity—enough to share—the A-3 made an ideal tanker aircraft. (US Navy.)

When NAS Whidbey's A-3s were not busy refueling aircraft from their own squadron, they served as tankers for the aircraft of others. Here, an A-3 of VAH-4 tops off an RA-5 of RVAH-13 while deployed with the USS *Kitty Hawk* (CVA-63) to Vietnam in 1965. Both aircraft in this photograph were later shot down during the Vietnam War. (US Navy.)

Despite the rigors of war, life at NAS Whidbey went on. A popular way to spend a Saturday night was attending one of the dances held at the Chief Petty Officers Club. In a building greatly expanded over the years, the club continues to serve as a venue for various functions and is the site of many happy memories. (NAS Whidbey Chief Petty Officers Club.)

Although this photograph is undated, the sign on the guard shack places it in 1961, when the Navy celebrated "50 Years of Naval Aviation." The hospital is on the right, and a banner reminds sailors that it is time to "help a shipmate" and donate to the Navy Relief Society. (US Navy.)

The early 1960s Ault Field flightline should be easily recognizable to sailors of today. By that time, the layout of the base was far more practical than it had been only 10 years earlier. Major construction projects were yet to come, but the center of the base had been established. (US Navy.)

For many years, the UF-1 Albatross was a ubiquitous aircraft at NAS Whidbey. Primarily used for search and rescue, the Albatross (later renamed the HU-16) was amphibious and capable of landing just about anywhere. With its Day-Glo orange nose and empennage, the Albatross was a familiar sight as it patrolled the shores of Puget Sound. (US Navy.)

The Base Operations Building in the 1960s was as busy then as it is now. Whidbey's UF-1 Albatross is seen in the background, as are several World War II–vintage buildings. By the 1960s, the wooden barracks in the background were no longer used for housing and had been converted into office space. Three of these historic structures are still in use today. (US Navy.)

Since its earliest days, NAS Whidbey has always been active in community affairs. The base Honor Guard has appeared on countless occasions, and no Oak Harbor parade is complete without the Navy's participation. For the 1961 Memorial Day Parade, Miss NAS Whidbey, her court, and an A3D graced the city's streets. (Scott Hornung.)

One of the many things that made seaplane operations unique was the sheer practicality of how they operated. For most aviation-minded people, towing an aircraft brings to mind a tractor-type vehicle and a plane with wheels. With a seaplane, towing the aircraft usually meant getting a boat and a lot of rope. (US Navy.)

By the mid-1960s, the sun was setting for US Navy seaplanes. The world was still mostly covered in water, but runways had been built just about everywhere, and the range of the Navy's new P-3 Orion meant refueling stops at out-of-the-way places was no longer a factor. (US Navy.)

As seaplane operations at NAS Whidbey were beginning to wind down, the seaplane base settled into a well-earned rest. Even with the P5Ms, the west parking ramp shown here had been little utilized after World War II. The former nose dock was transformed into the auto hobby shop. The metal sheds behind it were originally used for storing torpedoes. (US Navy.)

An A-3 Skywarrior of NAS Whidbey's VAH-8 is shown far from home in the skies over Vietnam. Designed to haul a heavy 1950s nuclear bomb, the A-3 could carry an impressive payload of conventional weapons and deliver them day or night and in all kinds of weather. This plane was a true workhorse for the Navy. (US Navy.)

Four

THE INTRUDER AND PROWLER ERA

Another chapter in NAS Whidbey's history began when the Navy's newest attack aircraft, the two-seat A-6 Intruder, made its appearance in the skies over Oak Harbor in 1966. The US military's involvement in Vietnam was ever-increasing, and Whidbey's brand-new Intruders were in the thick of it almost from the day they arrived. (US Navy.)

The A-6 Intruder would never win a prize in a beauty contest, but it was rugged, dependable, versatile, and very advanced. With state-of-the-art electronics, its two-man crew of a pilot and a bombardier/navigator could deliver bombs and other ordnance with pinpoint accuracy in all weather conditions, day or night. (US Navy.)

In the mid- to late 1960s, NAS Whidbey was home to A-6 Intruders, A-3 Skywarriors, and the ageless P-2 Neptune. As the decade came to a close, Whidbey's maritime reconnaissance role seemed to be coming to an end as the VP squadrons began to depart. The future had different plans. (US Navy.)

NAS Whidbey continued its mission of training aircrew and maintenance personnel. Schools for the A-6 were quickly established, and the graduates were soon entering into the world of the Intruder. Even though beards and sideburns were in vogue for these recently minted A-6 maintenance men, their chief did not share in his students' taste for the latest hairstyles. (US Navy.)

Although 1965 marked the end for seaplane operations, 1966 saw the inauguration of the A-6 Intruder at NAS Whidbey. It was time for VP-47 and its P-5 Marlins to go, and an era ended with their departure; this was true of Whidbey Island, but also for an entire Navy that had always flown seaplanes. (US Navy.)

Another familiar sight at NAS Whidbey Island was lost for good when the USS *Salisbury Sound* departed in 1967. Even when the seaplanes left in 1965, Whidbey remained the homeport for the *Sally*. She made several deployments during 1965–1966 before she sailed for the last time to decommissioning in Bremerton in January 1967. (US Navy.)

NAS Whidbey continued to see improvements and developments during the late 1960s. New barracks were constructed to handle the increase in personnel that accompanied the A-6 Intruders. This parking lot in front of one of the new barracks, Building 380, is a classic-car aficionado's dream. (US Navy.)

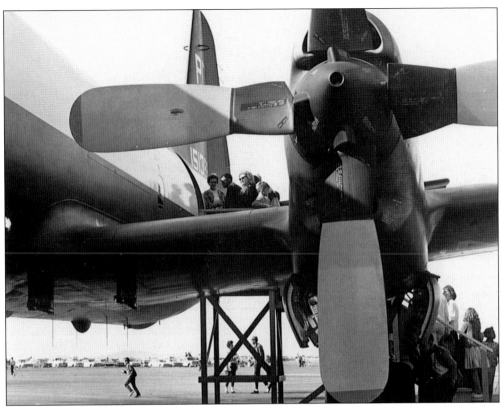

A new P-3A Orion of VP-9 attracts a crowd at an open house in the mid-1960s. Familiar to Whidbey Islanders since its arrival in 1975, the Lockheed P-3 is a military adaptation of Lockheed's Electra airliner and has been a true workhorse of the Navy. Although it is soon to be retired, in the hearts of many, it will never be replaced. (US Navy.)

These angora-clad women in front of Hangar 2 found a unique perspective from which to enjoy NAS Whidbey's open house and airshow in the mid-1960s. This annual event was a mainstay for many years. By 2001, security and budget constraints had sharply curtailed such events. (US Navy.)

Navy Relief Society graduates are presented with their certificates by NAS Whidbey skipper Capt. Beecher Snipes and the chaplain in 1966. With the hardships and losses of the Vietnam War, the services provided by Navy Relief were in great demand. Now the Navy–Marine Corps Relief Society (NMCRS), the organization continues to provide for sailors in need. (NMCRS.)

An impressive new chapel was built in 1962 and has continued tending to the religious and spiritual needs of NAS Whidbey ever since. Always busy with weddings and christenings, the chapel also holds dignified memorials to Whidbey sailors who have sacrificed their lives in the service of their country. (US Navy.)

With the seaplanes gone for good, NAS Whidbey began finding new uses for parts of the seaplane base. One such example was the construction of a state-of-the-art gas station. Operated by the Navy Exchange, this station is now gone, but another was built to take its place. (US Navy.)

As operations were consolidated at Ault Field, many of the functions located on the seaplane base were relocated. One was the hospital, which was replaced with a new facility in 1969. The old building had a new lease on life when it and the surrounding property were transferred from Navy hands to the state. The old hospital is now home to Skagit Valley College. (US Navy.)

A welcome addition to the NAS family in 1970 was the EA-6 Prowler. A four-seat electronic attack version of the A-6 Intruder, the Prowler clears a path for friendly strike aircraft by jamming enemy radar and electronics or destroying the radar sites themselves. Although the aircraft is still in service with the US Marine Corps, the last of Whidbey's Prowlers left in 2015. (US Navy.)

What an aircraft lacks in appearance is often made up for in its capabilities. This VAQ-134 Prowler carries a varied assortment of electronic equipment both visible and unseen. The bulges and bumps house antennae, and electronic warfare-related pods are carried under the wings and belly. (US Navy.)

A familiar sight—a Neptune—returned to NAS Whidbey when VP-69 was established in 1970. Flying the SP-2H Neptune, VP-69 was (and is) a squadron of the Naval Reserve. The prominent "stinger" protruding from the tail housed part of the aircraft's submarine detection gear. (US Navy.)

As the A-6s became operational, the A-3 squadrons of NAS Whidbey were decommissioned or redesignated and reequipped to become electronic attack squadrons. Typical of this transition was VAH-4, which traded its bomber version of the A-3 for electronic warfare models. It was redesignated VAQ-131. (US Navy.)

The A-3 did soldier on in various guises, including that of an aerial refueling aircraft designated the KA-3. Its role as a strictly attack aircraft was taken up by newer planes such as the Intruder and the A-7 Corsair II. Skywarriors served in an assortment of roles until the last was retired in 1991. (US Navy.)

When the A-6 aircrews were sufficiently trained and mission-ready, they were deployed to the Far East and Vietnam. A Whidbey-based Intruder from VA-165, the "Boomers," is being loaded for bear on the deck of the USS Ranger (CVA 61) as it is made ready for another mission in the dangerous skies over Vietnam. (US Navy.)

VA-52, the "Knight Riders," was a longtime NAS Whidbey A-6 Intruder squadron. Arriving at Whidbey in 1967, the Knight Riders soon transitioned to the A-6 and made some of the initial Intruder deployments to Vietnam. The squadron stayed at Whidbey until it was decommissioned in 1995. (US Navy.)

As NAS Whidbey entered the 1970s, there came new changes to the station and Ault Field. The World War II hangars were slowly replaced by more modern structures, and parking space on the ramp was expanded to provide a more suitable home for the patrol aircraft of VP-69. (US Navy.)

NAS Whidbey's A-6s often sported very attractive and attention-getting markings during the 1960s and 1970s. This aircraft, the personal mount of the commander of VA-95, was no exception and was especially eye-catching. VA-95, the "Green Lizards," was based at NAS Whidbey during the early 1970s. (US Navy.)

Although these are hardly the skies over North Vietnam, these Intruders from Whidbey's VA-165 are loaded up with about as many MK-82 500-pound bombs as they could carry. One of the A-6's great strengths was its ability to haul just about anything the Navy could think to attach to an aircraft. (US Navy.)

A well-known NAS Whidbey alumni is Stephen Coonts, naval pilot and bestselling author of *Flight of the Intruder, The Cannibal Queen,* and dozens of others. Coonts (right), shown here upon his completion of training in the A-6 with Whidbey-based Attack Squadron 128 (VA-128) in 1970, went on to serve two tours in Vietnam flying combat missions off the USS *Enterprise.* (Stephen Coonts.)

The deployment cycle for the A-6 was a fast one, with crews constantly coming and going. Both the air and maintenance crews seemed to spend a good deal more time on an aircraft carrier than not. VA-115, the "Arabs," was an early Intruder squadron from NAS Whidbey. (US Navy.)

Not too far from their base at NAS Whidbey Island, a four-plane formation of A-6s from VA-52 makes for an impressive display as they approach their home in the early 1970s. They would soon deploy to Vietnam and conduct the first air raids over North Vietnam since 1968. (US Navy.)

Certainly one of the oddest looking aircraft ever to be assigned to NAS Whidbey was the TC-4C Academe. A Grumman Gulfstream with the addition of an A-6 Intruder nose, a simulated A-6 cockpit, and consoles for bombardiers and navigators, the TC-4C was used for training Intruder crews. (US Navy.)

In the post–Vietnam War years, NAS Whidbey's Intruders came back to their island home and resumed operations. Despite the relative calm of the 1970s and 1980s, there were situations and trouble spots in the world that required the use of military force, and Whidbey A-6s were utilized. (US Navy.)

The C-1 and S-2 are two of the lesser-known aircraft in NAS Whidbey's historical inventory. Both aircraft were assigned to the Naval Air Reserve Unit (NARU) and performed a variety of missions and purposes. Both served at NAS Whidbey until the early 1980s. (Author's collection.)

A fully loaded A-6 Intruder is always an impressive sight, especially when the aircraft is waiting to be shot into the air from a catapult on an aircraft carrier. The location pictured here is off the coast of North Vietnam; the bombs weigh 500 pounds each. (US Navy.)

Not every landing is as successful as the last. The crew of this VAQ-129 EA-6B Prowler experienced a rather eventful arrival, but they landed safely—due in no small part to the longstanding professionalism of the NAS Whidbey Fire Department, which had rescue crews standing by. (US Navy.)

The A-6 Intruder also had its share of bad days. Failure to lower the landing gear is certainly not unique to the A-6, NAS Whidbey, or the US Navy, but it is always embarrassing. Happily, no one was injured in this mishap. (US Navy.)

From the day the air station opened in 1942, the safety of its aircrews has been paramount. That tradition is unbroken. In the 1970s and 1980s, the helicopter of choice for NAS Whidbey rescue crews was the HH-46 Sea Knight. Hangar 1, "SAR Country," was the longtime home for Whidbey's Search and Rescue helicopters. (US Navy.)

The search and rescue crews have always earned their well-deserved reputation within the US Navy. They tend to be quiet professionals whose motto, "So Others May Live," is at the heart of everything they do. The SAR crew's camaraderie, as shown here in the 1980s, is one of the keys to their success. (US Navy.)

The HH-46 was replaced by the smaller but extremely versatile SH-3 Sky King. Able to land where the larger HH-46 was unable to, the Sky King had the additional ability to land on water. Later renamed the UH-3, this helicopter served NAS Whidbey well and remained on the island until 2006. (US Navy.)

The P-2 Neptune's long association with NAS Whidbey seemed to be coming to a close when that aircraft departed in the late 1960s, but when VP-69 was established in 1970, the Neptunes once again returned. Other Whidbey VP squadrons converted to the P-3, but their stay was short-lived. By 1970, only VP-69 remained. (US Navy.)

In 1975, NAS Whidbey said a final goodbye to the P-2 Neptunes when VP-69, "The Totems," converted to the P-3 Orion. This was the second time P-3s had been based at Whidbey, but the other squadrons had flown the aircraft for only a brief time before they transferred to other air stations. (US Navy.)

VP-69 has flown the P-3 for over 40 years. As a Naval Reserve squadron, they are considered by some to be "Weekend Warriors." Nothing could be further from the truth: VP-69 is as busy as any active duty unit. Personnel often remain with the squadron until they retire at age 60 and have more hours in the P-3 than most of their active-duty counterparts. (US Navy.)

As helicopters took over the search and rescue mission, it was time to say farewell to NAS Whidbey's last seaplane, the HU-16 Albatross. The amphibious craft usually operated from the runways of Ault Field, but after a rescue, it would often land in the waters of the seaplane base due to the hospital being located there until 1969. (US Navy.)

Getting the latest weather, filing a flight plan, and checking the NOTAMs (Notice to Airmen) is daily routine at NAS Whidbey Operations. It was no different in the 1970s; only the haircuts have changed. In that era of long hair, the Navy reflected the styles of the time. (US Navy.)

EA-6B Prowlers of VAQ-134 are shown over Ault Field in the break for Runway 13. The Prowler had a long time to go at NAS Whidbey when this photograph was taken in the late 1970s. VAQ-134 was one of the Navy's last EA-6B squadrons and made the Navy's final Prowler deployment in 2014. (US Navy.)

The A-6s of VA-128 form a backdrop for the sailors of NAS Whidbey. By the time this photograph was taken in the late 1980s, the Intruder had been part of Whidbey for 20 years. Little did anyone realize that within a few years, the fate of NAS Whidbey would be uncertain. (US Navy.)

Five

NEW BEGINNINGS

The local community was stunned when, in 1991, NAS Whidbey was recommended for closure. Upon review, this recommendation was not acted upon. Instead, the island would become home for all the Navy's P-3s on the West Coast. With this new lease on life, a new era dawned at NAS Whidbey Island. (US Navy.)

One of the reasons NAS Whidbey was marked for closure was the Navy's decision to retire the A-6 Intruder fleet. The end of the Cold War necessitated a smaller Navy, and budget cuts were forthcoming. As it was, NAS Whidbey stayed open, and its Intruders maintained their local presence. (US Navy.)

When the newly arriving P-3 Orions appeared in 1993, they were certainly no stranger to the skies of Whidbey Island. Briefly stationed there in 1969–1970, and the airframe of choice for Whidbey's VP-69 since 1975, the P-3s smoothly transitioned into their new home. (US Navy.)

Although new types of aircraft were arriving and NAS Whidbey was adjusting to its new role, some familiar and older craft remained. One such familiar aircraft was the SH-3 Sea King helicopter (left). It flew until 2006, when it was retired in favor of the new SH-60 Seahawk (right). The SH-60 Seahawk was another welcome addition to the NAS Whidbey team. Dependable, fast, and capable of performing a multitude of missions day or night in all kinds of weather, the SH-60 and its crews have been called upon to participate in many hazardous rescue operations. (US Navy.)

NAS Whidbey's VAQ-134 had a lot to cheer about when, in 2002, the US Naval Academy football team defeated arch-rival Army. Spirits were running high at NAS Whidbey, but a sobering reality was the War on Terror that had begun the previous year. Whidbey personnel were already deployed to Afghanistan and other trouble spots, there to do their part to combat the latest threat to world peace. (US Navy.)

The pilot of an EA-6B Prowler conducts his "walk around" inspection before flight in the late 1990s. The protrusion from the nose strut is utilized for catapult launches on an aircraft carrier. The pilot is from the 27th Fighter Wing of the US Air Force. The end of the Cold War saw more joint training and operations among the different branches of the US military. (US Navy.)

It was almost unthinkable that the Air Force would call a naval air station home, but that was one of the many changes that have occurred at NAS Whidbey since the 1990s. Although accustomed to flying aircraft such as the F-15E shown behind these men, Air Force crews at Whidbey flew the EA-6B and, later, the EA-18G. (US Navy.)

Comdr. William C. "Willie" McCool, Prowler pilot and NASA astronaut, was twice stationed at NAS Whidbey. Piloting Space Shuttle *Columbia* on its ill-fated 2003 flight, McCool and the crew of mission STS-107 lost their lives when *Columbia* disintegrated on re-entry. Commander McCool is shown in this 1989 photograph while aboard USS *Coral Sea* (CVA-43) as a pilot in VAQ-133. (US Navy.)

Commander McCool was not the only astronaut to call Whidbey home. In the early 1950s, Comdr. (then ensign) Malcolm Scott Carpenter was assigned to NAS Whidbey as a young pilot in the P2V Neptunes. As one of the "Mercury 7," America's first seven astronauts, Carpenter was the fourth American in space and the second American to orbit the earth. (NASA.)

High over the Outlying Field at Coupeville, Navy parachutists hop out the back of a C-130 while taking part in a training mission. OLF Coupeville, built in 1943, has been part of Whidbey life longer than most can remember. It continues in service today as an invaluable training aid for the US Navy. (US Navy.)

After 30 years of service in the skies above Whidbey Island, the A-6 Intruder flew off into the sunset. Over the years, Whidbey's A-6s had served in Vietnam, the Gulf War, and in countless other global hotspots. It was a sad farewell when VA-196, Whidbey's last Intruder squadron, was decommissioned in 1997. (US Navy.)

In 2011, the Navy pulled out all the stops for its official commemoration of the Centennial of Naval Aviation. Several NAS Whidbey aircraft, including this EA-6B from VAQ-129, were given special paint schemes for that celebratory year. The markings represent those worn by the US Navy during the Battle of the Coral Sea in 1942. (US Navy.)

Another of Whidbey's squadrons was VQ-2. After arriving in 2005, VQ-2 flew the EP-3E in a variety of reconnaissance and intelligence-gathering missions. In 2011, the Centennial of Naval Aviation prompted VQ-2 to paint one of its aircraft in vintage colors—in this case, the original paint scheme for a P-3 of the 1960s. (US Navy.)

The P-3 Orion has long been the gold standard for maritime reconnaissance aircraft. Since entering service in 1962, the Orion has taken part in every aspect of US military involvement. Starting as the P3V-1 and continuing through many models and modifications to the present day, it is slated for retirement in 2020. (US Navy.)

A new face at NAS Whidbey Island is the EA-18G Growler. Like its predecessor, the EA-6B Prowler, the EA-18G has a mission based in electronic warfare. One of the first to arrive in 2008 is shown in front of Operations parked near an EA-6. A C-9 from VR-61 is parked in the background. (US Navy.)

As more of the new Growlers arrived, it was only a matter of time before the Prowlers departed, and 2015 marked the end of over 40 years of EA-6B Prowler operations at NAS Whidbey Island. From the skies of Vietnam to those of Iraq and Afghanistan, the Prowler had been there and done that. (US Navy.)

The EA-18G Growlers arrived at NAS Whidbey over a span of seven years. During the 2011 celebration of the Centennial of Naval Aviation, the Growler got the same special treatment as other Whidbey aircraft, receiving this 1944 blue-and-white paint job. The Growler will be around for a long time to come. (US Navy.)

Flying formation with the P-3 in the background is the Navy's future aircraft for the maritime reconnaissance mission: the Boeing P-8 Poseidon. First arriving at NAS Whidbey in October 2016, the Poseidon will eventually take over the role and missions of the P-3 Orion. (US Navy.)

NAS Whidbey Island's past, present, and future are symbolized by the aircraft in this 2016 photograph: veteran P-3 types stand alongside the more modern C-40 Clipper, EA-18 Growler, and SH-60 Seahawk. The base has come a long way since 1942, yet memories are timeless for those who once called NAS Whidbey Island home. The legacy of NASWI has been passed to the Whidbey sailors of today and tomorrow. (US Navy.)

ABOUT THE PBY-NAVAL AIR MUSEUM

Located in downtown Oak Harbor, Washington, on Whidbey Island, the PBY-Naval Air Museum is operated by the PBY Memorial Foundation. Established on September 22, 1998, the foundation is dedicated to collecting, preserving, and presenting the history of all PBY Catalina aircraft, the aviation history of NAS Whidbey Island, and the role of naval aviation in the history of the Whidbey Island and Puget Sound communities.

Born as an idea during luncheon meetings of former PBY aircraft crews, the PBY-Naval Air Museum began humbly in a vacant gas station in downtown Oak Harbor. The passion and hard work of the museum's plankowners attracted the attention of NAS Whidbey Island's commanding officer, who arranged to bring the museum onto the air station in 2008. Subsequently, to accommodate growth and provide broader public access to the museum, it became necessary to move back into town and a larger facility. As this book goes to press, further growth and success is leading the PBY-Naval Air Museum to pursue construction of a larger, modern hangar-style museum in the Oak Harbor area.

As part of the PBY-Naval Air Museum's commitment to collecting and preserving the region's naval aviation history, it has embarked on a variety of projects including oral and video interviews, digitizing of documents and photos, collaboration with local libraries and museums, and supporting the publishing of books like the one you have in your hands. We are proud to collaborate with Arcadia Publishing and Will Stein in presenting this pictorial history of NAS Whidbey Island.

The PBY-Naval Air Museum's support of this book is dedicated to all who came before us and all who will follow.

DISCOVER THOUSANDS OF LOCAL HISTORY BOOKS FEATURING MILLIONS OF VINTAGE IMAGES

Arcadia Publishing, the leading local history publisher in the United States, is committed to making history accessible and meaningful through publishing books that celebrate and preserve the heritage of America's people and places.

Find more books like this at
www.arcadiapublishing.com

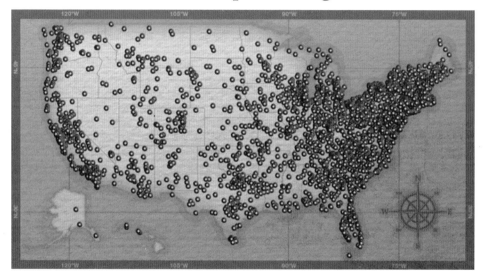

Search for your hometown history, your old stomping grounds, and even your favorite sports team.